WRITING AND IMPLEMENTING A MARKETING PLAN

Richard F. Gerson, Ph.D.

A FIFTY-MINUTE™ SERIES BOOK

CRISP PUBLICATIONS, INC.
Menlo Park, California

WRITING AND IMPLEMENTING A MARKETING PLAN

Richard F. Gerson, Ph.D.

CREDITS
Editor: **Nancy Shotwell**
Designer: **Carol Harris**
Layout and Composition: **Interface Studio**
Cover Design: **Carol Harris**
Artwork: **Ralph Mapson**

Copyright © 1991 by Crisp Publications, Inc.
Printed in the United States of America

Distribution to the U.S. Trade:

National Book Network, Inc.
4720 Boston Way
Lanham, MD 20706
1-800-462-6420

Library of Congress Catalog Card Number 90-84077
Gerson, Richard F.
Writing and Implementing a Marketing Plan
ISBN 1-56052-083-3

ABOUT THE AUTHOR

Richard F. Gerson, Ph.D., is president of Gerson Goodson, Inc., a marketing and management services firm that provides consulting services to small business owners, entrepreneurs, private practice service providers, and other consultants. The focus of his company's efforts is to develop marketing plans along with techniques to implement those plans successfully.

Dr. Gerson began his career as a business consultant and corporate trainer in the health care field. His client list has expanded to include businesses from a wide variety of industries. Dr. Gerson may be reached by writing or calling:

Richard F. Gerson, Ph.D.
Gerson Goodson, Inc.
P.O. Box 1534
Safety Harbor, Florida 34695
Telephone: (813) 726-7619

ABOUT THIS BOOK

Writing and Implementing a Marketing Plan is particularly useful for small business owners and service providers. It is a resource for anyone who knows the value of a written marketing plan and the necessity of revising that plan on a regular basis. No business should be without a business plan and a marketing plan.

This book is divided into three parts. The first briefly covers the elements of a business plan by providing an outline of its table of contents and a short description of each section. The second focuses on the basics of writing a good marketing plan. The third part of the book covers a variety of methods to implement the plan.

Do not try to rush through this book. Read it carefully. Take notes. Think about what you are doing to market your business. Wouldn't you like to compete on a higher level and achieve the same results as if you had a large marketing budget? Wouldn't you like to attract and keep new customers and increase your market share without spending much money? This book will provide you with the means to do that, and more.

TABLE OF CONTENTS

P A R T

I

The Business Plan

CHAPTER 1: PRE-PLANNING FOR SUCCESS

You can virtually guarantee your success in any business if you know who you are, what your customers want, where you are going, how you will get there, and what you will do once you arrive. The best way to achieve these objectives is to do some pre-planning before you begin writing your marketing plan.

The pre-planning phase requires you first to write a mission statement. A mission statement tells everyone who you are and what you will do.

How do you write a mission statement? It is really very simple. Just think of how you would define or explain your business to someone who asked you what you do. The answer can be your mission statement. Or, your mission statement can be in the form of a goal or an objective, something you want the business to continually strive to achieve.

SAMPLE MISSION STATEMENTS

These examples of corporate mission statements will help you write your own. The first is the statement for my company, Gerson Goodson, Inc. We are a marketing and management services firm providing training and consulting advice. Our mission statement is:

> "To be a growth-oriented company who guarantees the satisfaction of its clients through the provision of high quality marketing and management consulting and training services. (that benefit the clients both personally and professionally.)"

The Marriott Corporation is one of the premier hospitality companies in the world. It is known for customer service and relations. This mission statement is posted in many of their hotels:

> We are committed to being the best lodging and food-service company in the world by treating employees in ways that create extraordinary customer service and shareholder value.

COMPUTERPEOPLE is a leading personnel services firm specializing in the placement of data processing experts in the state of Florida. Although this mission statement appears lengthy, it represents a combination of the various types of statements.

> COMPUTERPEOPLE will remain Florida's leading personnel services firm specializing in data processing and computer professionals. We will provide our clients with contract personnel for short or long assignments with an optional conversion of contract personnel to the client's permanent staff. In addition, COMPUTERPEOPLE provides recruiting services for the placement of permanent employees. The company will maintain its position by providing clients with well-trained and highly qualified candidates and guaranteeing their placement with superior customer service and total client satisfaction.

Practice writing a mission statement for your business below.

_____

_____

_____

_____

_____

You may also want separate mission statements for your marketing efforts, your customer service philosophy and your employees. The following statements can be applied to any company in any industry with minor modifications.

Marketing: To increase annual market share by 5% each year through innovative and creative marketing and promotional programs.

Service: To respond quickly to customer needs and recommendations and to do whatever it takes to satisfy the customer.

Employees: To develop pride of ownership and a high level of job satisfaction in each employee through training, recognition, rewards and empowerment so they will guarantee the satisfaction of every customer.

Once you have developed these four written mission statements, you are ready to begin the second phase of your pre-planning process. This is a direct question and answer session you must have with yourself and your employees. I call it a Market Business Analysis, or MBA. This MBA will help you get ready to write and implement your business and marketing plans.

MARKET BUSINESS ANALYSIS

What is the mission/nature of the business?

What corporate image does the business have?

What are the products/programs/services the business offers?

Who are the customers and where are they located?

What are their primary needs and desired benefits?

What unique positioning does the business hold?

Who are the competitors and what is their market share?

What are the most effective promotional tactics?

When and how will the products/programs/services be distributed?

What are the resource requirements for the business?

CHAPTER 2: WRITING THE BUSINESS PLAN

It is best to develop the business plan before writing the marketing plan, as the marketing plan is an outgrowth of the Marketing Analysis section of the business plan. The contents of the business plan are shown in outline form below.

I. EXECUTIVE SUMMARY
1. General description of the business plan
2. Introduction to the company
3. Brief description of the marketing program
4. Business and financial goals and requirements

II. COMPANY ANALYSIS
1. SWOT analysis
2. Company history
3. Product, program and service offerings
4. Prospective target markets and customers
5. Technology and resources
6. Major competitors and competitive position
7. Success factors
8. Cost comparisons

III. INDUSTRY ANALYSIS
1. Definition and description of the industry
2. Growth rate and key growth factors
3. Financial operating characteristics
4. Industry product life cycle

IV. MARKET ANALYSIS
1. Market scope
2. Market segmentation
3. Market barriers
4. Market demand
5. Market share and market sales
6. Distribution channels and sales approaches
7. Price structures and policies
8. Advertising, public relations and promotional plans

V. STRATEGIC ANALYSIS
1. Goals and objectives
2. Key performance/success indicators
3. Tactical plans and goal completion schedule
4. Operating assumptions

VI. MANAGEMENT ANALYSIS
1. Identification of key management personnel
2. Personnel pro forma for current and future needs
3. Organizational structure
4. Management and customer service philosophies

VII. FINANCIAL ANALYSIS
1. Budgets and pro formas
2. Financial schedules and financial statements

SECTIONS OF THE BUSINESS PLAN

Section 1: Executive Summary

The Executive Summary briefly describes the entire business plan. It should be no more than three to four pages in length and is usually written after the plan is complete.

Section 2: Company Analysis

This is an in-depth analysis of your company, beginning with a SWOT analysis. This stands for (Strengths, Weaknesses, Opportunities, and Threats) and it is best performed by using the chart on page 17. The company analysis also describes who you are, how you started, what you offer, and who your major competitors are. Finally, the company analysis includes the costs you will incur in running the business as compared to your competitors .

Section 3: Industry Analysis

The Industry Analysis describes your industry in depth. It identifies its growth rate, its financial operating characteristics, and where the industry is in its stage of life cycle development.

Section 4: Market Analysis

This is the section where you want to provide as much depth as possible. Market scope refers to how and where you offer your programs and services. Are you a local, regional, national or international company? Market segmentation is extremely important in that it determines how you will target your market. Targeting a market requires two steps. The first identifies the characteristics of the target market based on demographics, psychographics, or location. The second determines the attractiveness of the target market.

Once you know your target markets, you need to know what barriers there are to entering each marketplace, and what type of demand exists for your product or service. Include your current market share and sales volume, as well as the same figures for your top three competitors.

Next, you must determine if your sales and distribution channels are appropriate for this marketplace. What price structures are you offering customers? Finally, you want to give a brief mention of your promotional plans.

SECTIONS OF THE BUSINESS PLAN (Continued)

Section 5: Strategic Analysis

The Strategic Analysis section covers the goals of your business, your conceptual plans for performance, a description of the tactics you will use to succeed, a time schedule for that success, and a list of any operating assumptions that may apply.

Section 6: Management Analysis

The Management Analysis identifies your key personnel. Additionally, a personnel pro forma should be developed to project future staff needs. Your organizational chart is included in this section, along with management and customer service philosophies.

Section 7: Financial Analysis

The Financial Analysis describes the business from a financial standpoint. Budgets and pro formas are included in this section, along with other financial schedules and statements. Any special financial considerations for the operation of the business should also be mentioned here.

Follow the topic headings on the table of contents, combine them with the above descriptions, and you will be able to produce a comprehensive and formal business plan. This plan will guide you in writing the marketing plan.

P A R T

II

Writing
the Marketing Plan

Marketing is simply a beneficial exchange process between you and your customers. The key factor in this relationship is your ability to identify customer needs. It is up to you to develop the products or services that will satisfy those needs. The marketing process begins with an analysis of the types of markets that you want to focus on. It continues with the determination of how to get specific clients to purchase your products or services.

EXECUTIVE SUMMARY

The Executive Summary in the marketing plan is similar to the one you wrote in your business plan. It briefly describes the marketing plan, the product or service you offer, your target markets, the level of sales and profit margins you hope to achieve, and who your competitors are. You must also describe your marketing and promotional mixes, along with their associated strategies and tactics.

Many people will read the executive summary first. If this does not interest them, they will not read the rest of the plan. This can prove to be a disaster if you are presenting the plan to a banker or an investor for funding. Therefore, keep the summary section short, inclusive, and easy to read.

CHAPTER 3:
THE MARKET ANALYSIS

The market analysis section of the marketing plan uses much of the information in the same section of the business plan. The changes you will have to make include market research results, an identification of the level of attractiveness the market holds, where you are in the product life cycle, an in-depth look into your own company, your competitors, your customers, and your cooperators, and finally, an analysis of the product or service you offer.

Market Research

Market research is essential to the success of any business. It does not have to be expensive. A lot of information is inexpensive or free. For example, if you need census data on a particular neighborhood, you can go to your local library and ask for the information. This is an example of secondary research: the information you are using was gathered for another purpose. It is the least expensive type of market research.

The most popular types of market research include surveys, questionnaires and interviews. These are fairly easy to develop and analyze, especially if you want only a rough estimate of the percentage of people who feel a certain way about a product or service. When you collect this information yourself, it is called primary research, because it is directly related to what you are studying. While primary research is more expensive than secondary research, it does not have to be cost prohibitive.

MARKETING ANALYSIS (Continued)

The important thing is to do market research on whatever you are trying to sell. One of the biggest mistakes a business can make is to neglect to test the marketplace for its product or service.

This section of the marketing plan describes the results of your market research. It should be a brief summary of what was done and what was accomplished. It should not be as comprehensive as a separate market research report. The results of your market research should also relate to the rest of the market analysis section.

Market Attractiveness

This section describes how attractive the market is. Can customers afford your product or service, will they buy it, and can they refer new customers to you? These are just some of the questions you must answer in this section. To help you, use the brief scale on the following page to rate how attractive the market is to you. The higher your total score, the better your chances of succeeding in that marketplace.

TARGET MARKET ATTRACTIVENESS
RATING SCALE

CRITERIA	ATTRACTIVENESS				
	LOW				HIGH
Market Size	1	2	3	4	5
Market Growth Potential	1	2	3	4	5
Client Accessibility	1	2	3	4	5
User Potential	1	2	3	4	5
Payment Capabilities	1	2	3	4	5
Entry/Exit Potential	1	2	3	4	5
Competition	1	2	3	4	5
Referral Potential	1	2	3	4	5
Service/Program Awareness/Recognition	1	2	3	4	5
Service/Program Need	1	2	3	4	5

Product Life Cycle

Every product or service goes through four stages. These four stages are introduction, where the offer is new and there are very few or even no competitors; growth, where people are aware of and purchase the offer so the company earns high revenues; maturation, where many companies compete and some companies are even looking to get out; and decline or exit, where there is no longer a need for the product or service and the best business decision would be to sell it off or discontinue it.

MARKETING ANALYSIS (Continued)

Each stage is characterized by different marketing strategies and tactics. For example, in the introductory stage, you can charge very high prices for your offer because you are probably the only game in town. However, as the cycle moves into the maturation stage, more players are in the game and the demand for your offer may be dropping. Therefore, you may have to lower your prices or develop a new use for your product or service in order to remain competitive.

Company Analysis

Your success in business depends on knowing your company inside out. Use the SWOT Analysis chart on the following page to identify your strengths, weaknesses, opportunities and threats. Strengths are those things you do well and that set you apart from competitors. Weaknesses are the areas you have to improve upon, especially if you do not want your competitors to capitalize on them. Opportunities include everything that can benefit your business, such as an increased customer base, other businesses closing their doors, or special promotions that only you can offer. Threats are those things that can hurt your business, like a major competitor opening next door, a price increase from your suppliers, or your employees going on strike.

Identify all these characteristics of your business, and anything else that you can think of that affects its operation. Analyze your competitors to identify where they are strong, where they are weak, and where you can capitalize on areas that they have left open to you.

SWOT ANALYSIS

STRENGTHS	WEAKNESSES

OPPORTUNITIES	THREATS

MARKETING ANALYSIS (Continued)

Competitor Analysis

While it is essential to know your competitors, knowing them does not guarantee your success. You must still be able to carry out the tactical action plans that you will develop to market your business.

The competitor analysis begins with a SWOT analysis of your top three competitors. Then compare certain characteristics of each competitor to those of your business. The chart on the following page will help you get started.

Try to analyze their marketing mixes. If you know their marketing mixes, strategies and tactics, you can successfully compete with them.

To find information on your competitors, check out your local library. If you have a computer with a modem, one of the national bulletin boards with online services can probably provide you with all the information you need. Other ways for you to gather information on your competitors are shown under Competitor Information Sources in Appendix page 89.

COMPETITORS' COMPARATIVE CHARACTERISTICS

CHARACTERISTIC	YOUR COMPANY	COMPETITOR A	COMPETITOR B	COMPETITOR C
1. Geographic Boundaries				
2. Target Markets				
3. Market Segmentation Procedures				
4. Marketing Strategies and Tactics				
5. Marketing Assumptions				
6. Marketing Mix				
7. Program/Products/ Services Offered				
8. Operating Costs/ Assumptions				
9. Market Share				
10. Marketplace Entry/Exit, Stage of Life Cycle				

COMPETITOR ANALYSIS: MARKETING MIX

COMPETITOR'S NAME: _____ DATE: _____

PRODUCT/PROGRAM/SERVICE NAME:
    Production Costs:
    Supplier Relations:

PRICING STRATEGY:
    Leader/Follower:
    Price Position:

PLACE/DISTRIBUTION CHANNELS:
    Primary:
    Secondary:
    Distributor Relations:
    System Advantages/Disadvantages:

PROMOTION:
    Types:
    Quality/Effectiveness:

POSITIONING:
    Target Market/Niche/Segmentation:
    Unique Features/Benefits/Attributes/Uses:

SERVICE POLICY:
    Product/Program/Service Support:
    Customer Support:

Customer Analysis

It is essential to your success and the success of your marketing plan that you perform a customer analysis. You must know who your customers are, where they come from, what they will buy, how and when they will buy it, and what you have to do to keep them loyal to you. You can mention your customers briefly in this section, but I suggest you complete a more in-depth customer analysis in Section 3 of the marketing plan. This section is specifically designated to describe your customers and your target markets.

Cooperator Analysis

Few, if any, marketing plans provide an analysis of a company's cooperators. These include vendors, suppliers, outside salespeople, volunteers, or anyone who would cooperate with you to help make your business successful. Identify these people and companies in your marketing plan.

Product/Program/Service Analysis and Evaluation

The last portion of your market analysis identifies what you are selling to the consumer. The chart on the following page shows the areas of concern when evaluating your offering. Complete one chart for each product or service you sell. You will notice that the evaluation is almost like a mini-marketing plan. That is by design. It is intended to help you integrate your offerings into the whole scope of the marketing plan. In addition, this chart will provide you with a ready reference whenever you want to quickly evaluate your marketing efforts for a particular offering.

PRODUCT/SERVICE EVALUATION

MISSION STATEMENT/RATIONALE:

GOALS AND OBJECTIVES:

COMPANY STRENGTHS AND WEAKNESSES:

COMPETITOR STRENGTHS AND WEAKNESSES:

TARGET MARKET/UNIQUE POSITIONING:

COSTS/RESOURCES REQUIRED:

SERVICE AREA:

DISTRIBUTION METHODS:

CUSTOMER SERVICE PROGRAM:

EVALUATION TECHNIQUES:

TIME REQUIREMENTS:

CRITICAL ISSUES:

CHAPTER 4: MARKET SEGMENTATION AND TARGET MARKET SELECTION

This chapter can also be known as Customer Analysis because everything in it relates to your customers. This part of your marketing plan will help you determine who your customers are, where they are located, how and why they will buy from you, what makes them unique, and what you have to do to keep them loyal. The chapter is called market segmentation because this is the *only* way for a business to succeed in today's highly competitive environment.

The concepts of market segmentation and target market selection have become known as *niche marketing*. Niche marketing is simply defined as being a big fish in a little pond. Instead of trying to compete on a grand scale, businesses choose to compete in smaller areas. These are called niches. Within these niches, businesses must identify certain characteristics to differentiate customers from one another.

This is the process of segmentation, where two or more groups of customers have mutually exclusive and distinct characteristics. Once the market has been segmented, you can select your target market within your chosen segment. The marketing mix, strategies and tactics should be different and distinct for each of these segments.

Market Segmentation and Target Market Selection Criteria

Now you are ready to segment your market. Ask yourself, ''Is there a group of people being underserved in a particular area?'' For example, you may have heard people talking about not having a good place to go after a movie for coffee and dessert. If enough people in your area ''complain'' about this problem, you have found an underserved market segment.

You then have to determine if the target market within that segment has potential for you. You may want to review the target market attractiveness criteria you completed earlier. Or, you may want to determine if the target market can afford your services, if there is growth potential, who the competitors are, and the cost of doing business in this marketplace. You can take the process one step further by identifying the customer characteristics of your market segment.

TARGET MARKET SELECTION
(Continued)

Customer Analysis and Characteristics

Customers can be analyzed according to a variety of characteristics. The most common characteristics include geographics, demographics and psychographics.

Geographics, like geography, refers to where customers live or work. Demographics refers to such characteristics as age, income, gender, education, race, marital status, family size, occupation, culture, religion, job requirements, socioeconomic status and leisure activities. Psychographics refers to lifestyles, attitudes, values and beliefs.

You should consider many other characteristics when analyzing your customers. The chart on page 25 lists many of the things you must consider for your primary and secondary markets.

Your primary market consists of the customers with whom you do the most business. Your secondary market consists of customers with whom you do business, but either not as often or for not as much volume. Both these markets are important, and you should analyze them carefully. Even if they exist within the same market segment, you may have to develop separate marketing plans for them.

This point is critical to your success. When you have segmented a market and selected your customer targets on the basis of specific criteria, you must develop a separate marketing plan or program for each market.

TARGET MARKET CHARACTERISTICS

Characteristic	PRIMARY	SECONDARY
Location:	_____	_____
Age:	_____	_____
Gender:	_____	_____
Income:	_____	_____
Education:	_____	_____
Occupation:	_____	_____
Marital Status:	_____	_____
Family Size:	_____	_____
Family Life Cycle:	_____	_____
Buying Influences:	_____	_____
Benefits Sought:	_____	_____
User Status:	_____	_____
Usage Rate:	_____	_____
Loyalty Status:	_____	_____
Attitudes:	_____	_____
Readiness State:	_____	_____
Race/Religion/Nationality:	_____	_____
Lifestyle:	_____	_____
Social Class:	_____	_____
Personality:	_____	_____

TARGET MARKET SELECTION
(Continued)

Other Ways to Segment the Market

Several other categories or characteristics may be used to segment the market even further. The narrower you can make your marketplace, the more effective your programs will be. Some other primary market characteristics you may want to consider include:

Dollar Volume or Size—How much money can your participation in this marketplace generate? Are there enough potential customers to make it financially feasible for you to compete?

Sociopsychological Needs—What is the emotional state of the marketplace and does your product or service relate positively to that emotional state?

Purchaser/User Characteristics—Quite often, the user is not the purchaser, as when a parent buys children's clothing. You must know both the purchaser and the user.

Buying Influences—These include all outside people and events that can affect the purchase of your product or service.

Usage and Loyalty—Will your customers be loyal to your product or service? Try to find this out before settling on a particular market segment to do business in.

Getting to Know Your Customer

Many books discuss the importance of knowing your customers, but very few urge you to write a customer section in your marketing plan. Answer the following questions and then place them in this section of your marketing plan.

Who is my customer?

Is my customer male or female, married or single, white or blue collar, educated or not?

What does my customer need from me?

What does my customer want from me, and how does this differ from what s/he needs from me?

Can I satisfy those needs and wants, and if not, what changes must I make to satisfy them?

What does my customer expect from me in sales and service?

What must I do to meet and exceed those expectations?

Where will I find my customer?

What must I do to keep my customer loyal?

How do I get my customer to refer new customers to me?

What must I do to make sure that what I am selling is what my customer is buying?

These questions should help you get to know your customers. You can perform a SWOT analysis on your customers or interview several of them to find out who they are, why they do business with you, and what you have to do to keep their business. Put all this information into your marketing plan. It is as important as your demographic and statistical information.

CHAPTER 5: DEVELOPING THE MARKETING MIX

This is where the fun starts. In this section of your marketing plan, you develop strategies that will guide you toward success.

There are two preliminary steps you must take before developing the marketing mix. The first is to identify your overall goal or marketing strategy. The second is to identify your target audience. Then you can proceed to develop the marketing mix.

The typical marketing mix is based on the four P's: Product, Price, Place, and Promotion. These refer to the product or service you are selling, what it will cost the customer (price), where you will sell it or how the customer will receive it (place or distribution channels), and what communication techniques you will use to inform the public about your business (promotion).

Other factors you must consider when developing your marketing mix will increase the number of P's to eight, and add one S. The next P is Positioning, the unique place you hold in customers' minds. To position your business, ask yourself what is different or unique about you as compared to your competitors. Do you provide better quality, more product and value for the price, or do you simply fill an underserved need in the community? These are some of the ways to position your business.

Next is People. This represents the people who will work for you, sell your product or deliver your service and the vendors who will supply you. The last two P's are Profits, what you plan to make, and Politics, those laws and regulations that will govern the way you do business.

The S that everyone seems to forget about is Service. You cannot succeed today without providing excellent customer service. You must know who your customers are, what they need, want and expect, what you must do to satisfy those needs and wants while exceeding their expectations, and then have a system in place to resolve any customer complaints easily.*

Now that you know what goes into the marketing mix, you probably feel you are ready to develop one. Be patient. First, you must specify the performance goals for your business so that the marketing mix can help you achieve them. Since you already know who your target market is and what niche you want to serve, you can gear the marketing mix to those needs. Ask yourself what financial and other business goals, such as expansion or increased profit margins, you want to reach. Then develop the marketing mix in accordance with these goals and objectives. To help you establish these goals prior to the marketing mix, answer the following questions.

*Note: See Scott, *Customer Satisfaction,* and Martin, *Quality Customer Service* and *Managing Quality Customer Service,* all by Crisp Publications.

GOALS AND STRATEGIES FOR THE MARKETING MIX

What does the company want to achieve this year?

_____

_____

_____

How much money do we want to make? What is our desired profit margin?

_____

Where is the industry in the Product Life Cycle and what strategies are necessary to compete in this phase? _____

_____

Who is our target market and what is our unique position in their minds?

_____

_____

What is our time frame for achieving our business and financial goals?

_____

What resources do we have to implement the necessary tactics to achieve the strategies we develop in the marketing mix? _____

_____

Are there any specific legal ramifications or requirements related to our product or service? _____

_____

Do we have the required licenses, patents, trademarks and registrations for our product or service?_____

_____

Does our product or service infringe on any currently trademarked or registered product or service? If so, how will we overcome this obstacle?

_____

_____

DEVELOPING THE MARKETING MIX
(Continued)

1. Target market selection/market segmentation characteristics:

2. Products/programs/services offered:
   Name:_____

Features	Benefits	Need satisfaction

3. Distribution channels (accessibility and availability):

4. Price (includes discounts, incentives and payment terms):

5. Promotions:
   A. Types of communications:

   B. Techniques
      1. Advertising
      2. Publicity
      3. Public relations
      4. Business publications: brochures, flyers
      5. Direct mail
      6. Personal selling
      7. Telemarketing
      8. Networking
      9. Speeches
      10. Community service

Follow the form above to develop your own marketing mix.

Fill in one sheet for each product or service you offer. Every product or service, or every different market you serve, should have its own marketing mix.

Marketing Action Plans

Another simple device you may want to use to help you develop both your marketing mix and your promotional mix is the Marketing Action Plan, or MAP. It is a map of what you want to achieve and how you plan to do it.

The form below will help you develop your MAP. Design one MAP for each goal or strategy. Just fill in the form as it is set up. Remember that your goal is a nonspecific statement about what you want to achieve (similar to a strategy) and your objective is a very specific, behaviorally oriented and measurable statement of what you will achieve in a certain time frame. Your actions are the tactics you will use and the leader is the person responsible. The first letter of each word, Goal, Objective, Actions and Leader also spell out GOAL—just a reminder to keep you focused.

MARKETING ACTION PLAN

Goal:

Objective:

Actions:

Leader:

Comments:

NEXT TASK

You have now completed the marketing mix section of your marketing plan. Your next task is to develop the promotional mix. These are the tactics and actions you will implement to bring your marketing mix to life. The promotional mix will also serve as the basis for the last section of the book where we will discuss free and inexpensive techniques to successfully market your business.

CHAPTER 6: THE PROMOTIONAL MIX

The promotional mix consists of four parts. Advertising, which is paid media placements, is the one people are most familiar with. The next is public relations, which includes all publicity efforts. Many people think that public relations is free, but there are costs in staff time, program development time, and meeting the media. The third part of the promotional mix is personal or direct selling, which includes both face-to-face visits and telephone sales. The last part is sales promotion, which has to do with all your efforts to move your product or service at a discounted or special price.

Let's begin with advertising and discuss how you will include it in your marketing plan.

ADVERTISING

Since advertising is paid media space, either in print, on radio or television, the first question you must answer is whether or not you have the money to advertise. Media people will tell you that if you do not advertise, you cannot succeed. That is simply not true, as you will see in the next section of the book. Advertising is just one method of communicating about your business to the public.

If you advertise, you must develop the ads that you will place. It is best to keep a central theme for a time period. This way, people will become familiar with what you are offering. You may also want to consider hiring a professional to create your advertising campaign. Remember, though, that this campaign must be created in the context of your entire marketing plan with the sole purpose being to get you more customers. You do not want an advertising agency creating award-winning campaigns that do not sell your product or service.

THE PROMOTIONAL MIX (Continued)

Once you have your ads developed, you must prepare a monthly, quarterly and annual media schedule. These are the placements you will make in the various media. For example, you may use just newspaper one month, radio the next and television the third. Your media schedule will detail where the advertisement will appear, when it will appear, and, if possible, what it will cost. Whatever you do and however you advertise, code your ads in some way so that you can track their effectiveness.

It is not very effective to have ads that do not bring in business. If you are running multiple ads or using more than one media channel at a time, you need to know which ads are bringing in the business. That is why you have to code them. If it is a coupon, put a special number on it to indicate the date and newspaper it appeared in. If it is a radio or television ad, have the caller ask for a special person. These are just a few ways to track your ads.

You will want to include samples of your print ads and copies of your radio and television scripts in the documents section of the marketing plan. You will also want to keep an effectiveness rating (tracking effectiveness) of these ads, either in a separate file or in the marketing plan.

One final note about advertising. Some of the simpler methods include business cards, flyers, pamphlets and brochures. These will all be discussed in the next section of the book. Just because they are simple, commonplace and relatively inexpensive, you should not negate their advertising value and effectiveness.

PUBLIC RELATIONS

This is probably the most misunderstood part of the promotional mix. People think public relations is free, or at best, very inexpensive. That is their first mistake. Whenever you see a story about someone or some company, you can be sure that a great deal of time and effort went into getting that placement.

The second mistake people make about public relations is that they think just because a press release is sent into the newspaper, something will be printed. That is a fallacy. Although it is true that many pieces in the newspaper have come from press releases, the key is that the release discusses something newsworthy. Editors do not want to see self-serving press releases that are not newsworthy or do not benefit the community.

You should develop a public relations/press release schedule the same way you develop a media schedule for advertising. Include this in the marketing plan. Make certain, though, that when you send out the press releases, they contain news, not puff.

Keep the release to one or two pages. Identify it as a press release, either across the top or in the upper right hand corner. On the left side of the page, put the date the release was written, who the contact person is, and day and evening phone numbers. Then, come back to the right side of the page and put the date the release must be used by, or type ''For Immediate Release''. Next, skip two spaces (your entire release should be double spaced) and put in the title, underlined.

The next line begins with the city and state of the release. As you start to write the release, be very specific. Put the who, what, when, where, and how in the first one or two paragraphs. The rest of the release goes from the specific to the general. Remember that editors will edit your release from the bottom up. So you must get everything that is important for you to say in the first two paragraphs. If the release continues on to a second page, put ''More'' at the bottom. At the end of the release, put either three # signs or the number 30 to show the reader the release is finished.

The following page provides you with a sample press release that adheres to the above format and guidelines. Adapt it for your needs.

NEWS RELEASE

DATE: November 1, 1989
CONTACT: Richard Gerson
TELEPHONE: 726-7619

FOR IMMEDIATE RELEASE

RICHARD GERSON TO SPEAK AT INTERNATIONAL MEETINGS

Safety Harbor, Florida—Dr. Richard Gerson, president of Gerson Goodson, Inc., a marketing and management services firm, will speak at several international conferences in early 1990. Dr. Gerson, who is well-known for his presentations and publications in marketing and customer service, will deliver six seminars in four days in February 1990.

The first series of presentations will be four workshops for the Sporting Goods Manufacturer's Association Supershow, the largest gathering of sporting goods manufacturers, retailers, and buyers in the world. Dr. Gerson will present two seminars on effective and inexpensive marketing techniques and two on customer service programs and delivery systems on February 23 and 24, 1990, in Atlanta, Georgia.

Dr. Gerson will also present ''Customer Service: The Profit Strategy of the 90's'' at the largest gathering of professional fitness instructors, called APEX, on February 23, 1990.

His final presentation on February 25, 1990, also at APEX, will be ''Marketing and Sales Training.''

For more information about the content of these speeches, or any other services provided by Dr. Gerson, call him at (813) 726-7619.

#   #   #

DIRECT OR PERSONAL SALES

This part of the promotional mix in the marketing plan describes your personal sales efforts. It can refer to you personally or to your sales staff. It shows the reader to whom you are going to sell and with what kind of approach. You can also include the number of calls you want your salespeople to make on a daily, weekly, or monthly basis. I strongly recommend that you include at least an outline of your sales presentation, as well as the sales forms the staff is required to complete. If you do not want to put the forms in this section, you can place them in the documents section. In any case, these forms should be included somewhere so the reader of your marketing plan will know how you plan to stay informed about the personal selling efforts.

Telemarketing or telesales and direct mail are other forms of direct selling. If you are going to use these methods, describe what you will be doing in this section of the plan. Include samples here or in the documents section. Remember that only you can decide if a personal sales call is necessary for your business or if telephone sales or direct mail is more effective.

SALES PROMOTIONS

Sales promotions are the special programs you will offer the public to sell more of your product or service. They are usually time constrained, such as using a coupon by a certain date. Sales promotions are also used to move products that tend to be slow sellers, are going out of season, or are temporarily overstocked. Service providers often use sales promotions to create new business or entice former clients back into the business.

PROMOTIONAL MIX (Continued)

Sales promotions take many forms, and you must decide which is best for your business. The most popular promotions are a discount coupon for your product or service or a special offer for a particular time period. If you use either one, just make sure the promotion expires at a certain date so you can track its effectiveness.

CREATIVE DEVELOPMENT PLAN

This last section of the promotional mix is more of a check on both the marketing mix and the promotional aspects of the marketing plan than it is an integral part of the written document. Include it at this point in the plan to ensure that you have covered all your bases.

Your creative development plan requires you to answer a series of 10 questions related to each marketing opportunity. The questions are listed on the following page. When you complete this section, you can be assured that you have focused your marketing plan in general, and your marketing mix and promotional mix in particular, to your specific product or service for a given market.

The areas you will respond to in the creative development plan include identifying the marketing opportunity, your primary objectives, desired results, competitors and customers, the benefits you offer, your unique positioning, promotional tactics, measurement techniques, the constraints placed on your efforts, and any other critical factors that may affect the implementation of the marketing plan.

CREATIVE DEVELOPMENT PLAN

Project: Date:

Goal/Strategy:

Primary Tactics:

---

1. What is the key problem or opportunity?

2. What is the primary marketing objective to be achieved?

3. What results are expected from this marketing program?

4. Who are our target customers and competitors?

5. What benefits do we offer our customers?

6. What is our unique positioning or niche?

7. What promotional tactics will be used?

8. How will the effectiveness of the program be measured?

9. What constraints (budget, media, staff, etc.) exist for this program?

10. What other critical issues must be considered?

Your marketing plan is almost complete. You have analyzed your marketplace, identified your customers and competitors, determined your market niche, developed the strategies and tactics for your marketing and promotional mix, and now you probably think you are ready to implement the plan. Be patient just a while longer. You need to complete two more sections of the marketing plan before you implement it. The next section describes the marketing results you want to achieve through this plan. The last section is the marketing support documents section. When these are completed, you can move on to implementing the marketing plan effectively and inexpensively.

CHAPTER 7: MARKETING RESULTS AND SUPPORT DOCUMENTS

Marketing Results

Your evaluation procedures will be used to determine the effectiveness of the marketing plan. The evaluation procedures you select can include tracking responses to advertisements and sales promotion efforts, or they can be calculations of market share and market rank. Quite often, companies judge their success by their profit margins and relative competitive position in the marketplace. In other words, how do you compare to your top three competitors?

Relative market share is calculated by dividing revenues by the total gross revenues of your top three competitors. Your absolute market share is simply your revenues divided by the total revenues of your entire industry. Your market rank then becomes the rank order of your market share in relation to your competitors. The formulas below should make it easier for you to perform these calculations.

RELATIVE MARKET SHARE:

My Total Revenues/Revenues of Competitors A + B + C

ABSOLUTE MARKET SHARE:

My Total Revenues/Industry Total Revenues

MARKET RANK:

My market share in rank order with my top three competitors

This section on marketing results should also describe the sales goals you plan to achieve and your profit margins. Then, discuss how you will evaluate these efforts. If you have achieved your goals, what type of differential advantage do you now have? How have you solidified your unique positioning in the minds of your customers?

Support Documents

This seventh and last section is similar to an appendix. You include all your reporting mechanisms and sheets, such as sales call reports, advertising tracking forms and any other forms or charts. You also include copies of your marketing budgets, such as sales, income, expenses and advertising. You may even want to include sample ads and your media schedule if you did not include it in the promotional plan section. Finally, this section should include copies of contracts, approvals and any other legal documents related to the implementation of the marketing plan.

The Completed Plan

The marketing plan is now complete. It should be bound and reviewed carefully and regularly. This is a dynamic document that will guide you toward achieving your business goals. Writing the plan was not just an exercise; it was an integral part of your success. Therefore, make certain you refer to it and use it. Also, revise it whenever necessary. If you have a long-range strategic plan, your marketing plan should be exactly what you will do for one year of that long-range plan.

Now you must implement the plan in order to make your business successful. The third part of this book will introduce you to dozens of effective yet inexpensive marketing techniques that work. It is your responsibility to adapt them to your business. They have been proven across a wide variety of businesses, from retail to medical to professional services. They will work for you if you just take the time to apply them.

You may also want to go back to your tactics section of the marketing plan and revise it after you complete this part of the book. You can place the programs into your marketing plan. This would make your marketing plan even more complete.

WHAT'S IN IT FOR ME?

MARKETING PLAN

P A R T

III

Implementing the Marketing Plan

Your marketing plan comes to life when you develop the promotional tactics and activities to implement it. Most small businesses, however, and even some large ones, do not have extensive marketing budgets. Therefore, the implementation techniques presented in this section are relatively inexpensive. Some are even free. They all are effective.

The marketing techniques are presented in alphabetical order to make it easier for you to find the one you may be looking for. While the list is extensive, it is not inclusive. The goal here is to provide you with a variety of techniques you can use, as well as help you think of other techniques. In every case, you must adapt the suggestions to your situation.

MARKETING DEFINITION

ADVERTISING AGENCIES

Many small businesses create and place ads themselves because they cannot afford an advertising agency. If you form your own in-house agency with a slightly different name from your regular business, then you will be entitled to all agency discounts that the big companies receive, including the commission on placement.

If you are going to use an ad agency, make sure they present you with a marketing plan before they develop their advertising campaign. Or, make certain they have read your plan first. In either case, the marketing must drive the advertising. You must insist that the advertising they create for you will increase sales. The advertising campaign must be salesmanship in print. It is never enough to just win advertising awards if sales and profits do not increase. If that is all that is happening, it is time to change the ads or the agency.

ADVERTISING MEDIA

Advertising can be placed in print media, on radio, or on television. Most small businesses use their local newspaper, with some radio. Check your rates for each. You may even be able to use cable television at certain times of the day. Just make sure that if you advertise, you can afford the rates.

Print ads come in two types: classified or display. Display ads are the larger ads you see throughout the newspaper. They are the ones that are cluttered all over each other and make it hard to distinguish one from the other. If you are going to place a display ad, be unique and different enough, creative and innovative enough, so that the ad will stand out from the crowd.

ADVERTORIALS

Advertorials are paid advertisements in a newspaper or magazine that resemble an editorial or story. The client company writes what appears to be an article but places a notation at the top stating that the piece is an advertisement.

This is a very effective method of promoting your business, if you can afford to purchase the space. People read this material and often perceive it as an article. This gives you more credibility than a simple display ad. However, the advertorial often requires more space than other ads and can be more expensive. If you cram an advertorial into a small space, it looks crowded and becomes difficult to read.

Consider the tradeoffs if you plan to use advertorials. Are they cost effective for the response rate you will receive? How much do they add to your credibility?

ARTICLES

Publishing articles is a superb way to market yourself and your business, and increase your credibility in the minds of your customers. Where you publish the article is not that important. It can be a major newspaper, a small local paper, a magazine, a trade or professional journal. The important thing is to get the article published.

Make certain you write about your business or a topic related to your business. Remember that you want to use these articles to establish credibility and to inform the public about the product or service you offer. Try to get the article published where it will be read by the types of people you want to serve. Then, reprint the article and use it in your media kit.

AWARDS

Everyone likes to receive awards, and people like to do business with award winners. After all, if someone thought enough of you to give you an award for something, you must be a winner. Right?

Publicize your business-related awards in every way possible. Inform the press about your achievement. Place the plaques or trophies on display in your office in a conspicuous spot. Make certain everyone who enters your business can see them. If you are a professional such as a doctor, accountant, or lawyer, hang your diplomas and certifications in the reception room. Your clients and prospects will be impressed.

BALLOONS AND BLIMPS

One way to draw attention to your business is to fly a giant balloon over the location with a sales message on the balloon. Many businesses do this when they have a grand opening. You should even consider this at other times during the year. It is so conspicuous that people cannot help but notice your location.

Other businesses rent blimps to fly over the area with their messages. Some blimp companies will rent you advertising time or space. While this may be an intriguing and unique concept to promote your business, consider the cost, how many people will see the blimp and your message, and of those that do see it, how many will actually stop at your store or visit your office?

BARTER

This is a great way to market your business and not enough people take advantage of it. Basically, you are trading out your goods and services for the goods and services of a colleague. You both benefit. Bartering is the oldest form of trading and doing business. It fits in perfectly well with marketing since both are exchange processes. When you barter, determine if there is a cost involved. Also, check with your accountant to see if you must declare an income value for what you bartered or if the trade was equivalent for what you provided.

Barter as a marketing technique is very effective. It may not put money in the cash register, but it certainly can offer you many advantages over spending your own money. Consider it, and use it wisely.

BILLBOARDS

Billboards are probably the major form of outdoor advertising. Billboard rental is not cheap: some cost well over a thousand dollars a month. The billboard companies will help you design the board at no additional charge. They will also provide you with information on how many cars ride by your location each day and the basic demographics of the area. This information is intended to help you decide where to place your billboard.

If you use billboards, keep your message to seven words or less. People driving by at high speeds do not have time to read long messages. Also, make certain there is a telephone number or an address on the board. While people probably will not stop to write it down, at least they will have some idea how to reach you.

BOARD OF DIRECTORS

Establish a board of directors for your business. The board can be active or inactive. The idea is to seat people on your board who can help you in your business. Do not put family and friends on the board if they cannot bring you customers or leads or provide you with sound advice on how to run the business.

Many companies that have boards of directors do not use them to their fullest capacity. Yes, they may help you set policy. But as a marketer, you should view them as a resource. Whom do they know that they can introduce you to so you can start doing business? What other companies are they already doing business with that you are not? When can they introduce you?

You should ask influential people to sit on your board, and you should require them to bring one or two leads to each board meeting. Make it known that you will do the same for them. Use your board of directors to help you run your business and to expand your business.

BROCHURES

Brochures are an important part of any business. They convey your image and sales message and represent you when you are not personally present. They are a sales piece and an image builder. They keep you in the mind of your client or prospect. Therefore, if you want a business brochure, do it professionally, and hire a graphic artist and copy writer.

Too many businesses try to save money on their brochures, so they write the pieces themselves and have them quick printed. This serves no beneficial purpose and even costs you money in the long run. People will not want to do business with a company that promotes itself with a cheap or unprofessional-looking brochure.

Your brochure should offer a benefit in the headline or on the first panel. The copy should support that benefit and add value to it. Remember, the customer will buy what they perceive as a benefit and a value. Your brochure must tell them how what you offer will help them solve a problem or feel better.

BUDGETS

Have one! I cannot say it any simpler or more directly. Too many businesses never establish a marketing budget. They fly by the seat of their pants without ever knowing how much they are spending, what their return is, and what they are getting for the money.

BULLETIN BOARDS

Bulletin boards are a very effective marketing tool, and, quite often, they are free. Just look around in your local supermarket, a restaurant, or other businesses. Many places have bulletin boards where you can place your business card, a tear-off flyer or a brochure. The more bulletin boards you put your message on, the more people will begin to see it and recognize the name of your business. While you may not receive a great deal of business from placing a business card or flyer on an already crowded public bulletin board, you should expect a few calls. This will more than make the effort of placing the cards worthwhile.

You may also want to consider placing your business card or message on an electronic bulletin board that people access by computer. This inexpensive method of promoting yourself could get you a higher quality prospect list just because of the demographics of people who own computers, modems and use electronic bulletin boards.

One other suggestion, and this depends on your type of business. You may want to start your own bulletin board and allow people to place their messages. Some companies even have elaborate, professionally designed boards where they sell space. The space is not expensive, but it more than pays for the cost of the board. Plus, you end up getting a free placement because your costs are covered by your other advertisers.

Or, you may want to put a customer bulletin board in your office or business. This board lists customers' names and thanks them for their business or for referring people to the business. This type of referral bulletin board is used quite often by physicians and other professional service providers.

BUNDLING (PIGGYBACKING)

Bundling is a technique in which two or more products or services are sold as a package for less than the price of either alone. It is also used in direct mail when one company already plans to do a mailing, and another company places something in the envelope at a reduced cost. Another example of bundling is a two-for-one sale, or buy one, get one free, or buy one and receive the other item at half price. While these are all sales promotion techniques, they are actually variations of bundling.

Businesses will quite often bundle a slow-moving item with a better seller. This will help to clear their inventory as well as add perceived value to the sale. The public likes to buy when they perceive they are getting either added value or a deal. Bundling or piggybacking provides them with both.

BUSINESS CARDS

This is one of the most effective forms of marketing and is often the most abused. People do not pay enough attention to their business cards. You give out more business cards than anything else. Make certain that your card conveys your business message and the appropriate image.

You should not skimp on quality where your business cards are concerned. You should also make sure all the pertinent information is on the cards. The business name should be prominent. If you have a logo, put it on the card. Your name, title, business address and all telephone numbers, including fax and mobile, should be on the card. If people cannot reach you, how will you do business with them?

Give your cards out every chance you get. Believe that everyone who has your card is a potential customer or can refer a potential customer to you. If you feel funny about just giving someone your card, ask them for their card first. They will be glad to oblige, and then you can offer them your card.

One other point: multiply your marketing effectiveness by having business cards made up for your staff. Many companies do this, but they tend to skimp on these ''secondary'' cards, such as those for receptionists. Give the staff people the same quality cards you have. Spend the extra money on them. They will become your best sales people and give out more cards to more people than you could imagine or ever hope to give out alone.

GIVE EVERYONE YOU MEET A BUSINESS CARD!

BUSINESS MEALS

Some authors will tell you never to conduct business over a meal because the meal is distracting. I disagree. People have to eat, and if they do not want to hold a meeting over a meal, they will tell you. Otherwise, based on the type of business you have, you should invite clients and prospects to a business meal. And, since you do the inviting, you pick up the check.

Make certain you include business meals in your marketing plan and especially in your marketing budget. This is an effective way of helping people to relax, learning about their business and needs, and allowing you to close the deal.

CATALOGS

Catalogs are an excellent way to sell your product. However, they can be very expensive if you produce the catalog yourself. On top of that, you must add mailing list acquisition costs and postage. A more effective and less expensive method of selling through catalogs is to have your product included in someone else's catalog. You may have to pay them a small fee or a percentage of sales, but you will be better off in the long run. They have already tested their format and their lists. All you have to do is supply them with the pictures and fulfill the orders.

CHARITIES

This is an excellent way to gain a great deal of free publicity, visibility, community recognition, and credibility. Choose a charity to work with and then volunteer your time or donate products or services. You can inform the media about your actions. You should also be prepared to meet many other business people who are doing the same thing you are now doing: networking by assisting in a worthy cause.

CONFIRMATION CALLS

Confirmation calls are similar to a recall program in a professional practice. Basically, you are calling a customer (or a patient) to remind them of an appointment or a special sale. You want to make certain they come into your business. The confirmation call also makes them feel very special because it provides them with some value-added customer service.

CONTESTS

Contests are great ways to get people into your business. Contests can be sweepstakes, give-aways, promotional activities, or anything else that requires people to participate in your business where they can win something. The prize can be a free product or service, a trip, a membership in a club, or anything else you can think of. The purpose of the contest is to get people involved with your business and to keep them coming back for more. You can make the contest more effective by offering a ''Grand Prize'' to one winner and smaller prizes to other winners.

The success of the contest depends on its organization. You must consider how long the contest will run, how many people (approximately) will participate, what printed materials will be needed and what they will cost, how the information about the contest will be communicated to the public, the type, cost, and amount of the prizes, and how you will choose the winner(s). Not only will the contest itself generate good visibility and publicity for you, but the selection of the winner is also a newsworthy event.

CO-OP ADVERTISING

This is an often overlooked method of advertising. There are millions, perhaps billions, of dollars available every year for co-op advertising. Yet, businesses neglect to cash in on this source of advertising money, either because they do not know about it or they do not know how to go about getting the money.

Basically, co-op advertising is when you and one of your vendors or suppliers agree to jointly pay for an advertisement. Sometimes they pay you up front, sometimes they pay you after a certain amount of time has elapsed, and sometimes they pay you only after you spend a certain total dollar amount. They pay you to make their product name visible in your community.

The best way to receive money for co-op advertising is to ask for it. Tell the vendor about your marketing and advertising campaign and how it will benefit them. Your responsibility is to see that the advertising gets placed and the supplier's name is in the printed ad or mentioned on the radio or television.

There are two other forms of co-op advertising: Discretionary funding and vendor support. Discretionary funding requires you to send your supplier a proposal of your forthcoming marketing and advertising efforts. The proposal must include the exposure the supplier will receive from funding your effort. The supplier pays for the entire campaign, over and above any other monies that were designated for their own marketing campaign or co-op advertising.

In vendor support programs when the vendors contribute to a campaign, they receive mention in your advertising throughout the campaign. Vendor support is usually tied to one specific event, such as a grand opening, while discretionary funding usually is spread out over a larger time scale and campaign.

CO-OP REFERRAL LISTS

This is a simple arrangement between two or more non-competing businesses to trade their customer lists with each other. The purpose is to generate more business for each without taking business from each other. Co-op referral lists often result when you join a networking group or a leads club. This is one method of businesses using a reciprocal lead generation technique to help each other and their business.

COUPONS

This is a very popular form of sales promotion and one of the best ways to get people to try a new product or service. You can put coupons in a newspaper or magazine, on a flyer, as part of a brochure, in a coupon book. Other businesses may pay for the printing charges if you charge them a fee to be in the coupon book, or simply mail or hand them out themselves. The purpose of a coupon is to offer a trial discount so a new customer will do business with you.

Coupons are not that expensive to print. You should always offer a discount on the coupon, and remember to put an expiration date and a code of some type on it. The expiration date creates a sense of urgency and importance to use the coupon and the code lets you track the effectiveness and success of the campaign. Coupons are also a very effective method of marketing through cross promotions.

CROSS PROMOTIONS (JOINT VENTURE MARKETING)

Cross promoting your business with another simply requires both of you to agree to pass out information or coupons to your respective customers so that they will do business with your promotion partner. The three simplest methods of cross promotion involve exchanging coupons, flyers, or displaying each other's merchandise. Two other, although more complicated, methods involve refrigerator cards and value cards.

Refrigerator cards are promotions that you want the customer to paste on their refrigerator. The basic refrigerator card cross promotion involves two businesses who contribute to a 3" × 6" one-page flyer. One side has a description of your business with a coupon offer at the bottom. The reverse side has the same information about your partner's business, but the information and the coupons are in the opposite position. This is to prevent a customer from cutting out your coupon and destroying your partner's.

The value card is really an extension of the refrigerator card. This cross promotion involves six, eight, 10, or 12 businesses. Each business contributes a certain amount of money to the program and places their coupon on a 8.5" × 11" card stock paper. You then give each business 500 or 1,000 of these value cards. This gives you 1,000 × 9 or 9,000 other chances of having new customers come into your business, assuming there are 10 businesses on the card.

Another way to increase your exposure with a value card is to print on the back of each coupon, ''Compliments of...'', and list the 10 businesses. If you add it up, you will be getting 10 impressions (mentions) on the back of the card. If you print 10,000 cards, that is 100,000 impressions on the back and 10,000 on the front. Where else can you get 110,000 impressions for only an investment of a few hundred dollars or less?

CUSTOMER APPRECIATION PROGRAMS

A very simple customer appreciation program is a thank you card or note to new customers telling them you appreciate their business. Or, you can send the same thing to a customer who refers new business to you, thanking them for the referral. In fact, you should always do both.

Other types of appreciation programs include sending birthday and holiday cards to clients and customers. You can even send gifts to your extra special customers. This is done quite often around Christmas time, but you can also provide little, inexpensive gifts during the rest of the year to show them you care and appreciate their business. Calling your customers to remind them of an appointment or to follow up after they have called you with an inquiry or complaint goes a long way toward establishing customer loyalty.

CUSTOMER OF THE MONTH (OR YEAR)

This is a simple way to recognize your customers for their business. You simply purchase a plaque and each month put a customer's name on it, or give the winner an individual plaque. You must determine the selection criteria, but it can and should be very simple. For example, the customer of the month can be someone who refers the most new customers to your business, someone who purchases the most items or greatest dollar value, or someone who visits your facility and makes the largest number of purchases in a given month.

CUSTOMER SERVICE

You must strive to satisfy customers all the time. This means learning about and understanding their needs, wants, and expectations, and then doing whatever it takes to meet those needs and wants and exceed those expectations. You should always go the extra mile for your customers, especially if you are trying to rectify a complaint they have made. Remember that customers are the lifeblood of your business and the reason you are in business. You must do everything in your power to satisfy them. If you do not do this, your competitors will.

CUSTOMER SURVEYS

Surveys are an easy way to find out what your customers think about your business, its products and services. You do not have to spend a great deal of money to conduct these surveys. Some techniques include mailing written surveys to your customers and hoping they will respond and return them, telephoning them and asking them a series of questions, or giving them a card to fill out and mail back in.

An even simpler technique is to question them directly at the time they complete their purchase, or if they leave without making a purchase. What did they like or dislike? What else would they like to see? Were they satisfied? What else can you do for them? These are just some of the questions you should ask. You should use these surveys to solicit complaints from your customers. Then use the complaints as opportunities to improve your business.

Surveys provide a wealth of information to you. It is up to you to do something with that information so you can better market your business and service your customers.

DEMONSTRATIONS

Demonstrations are an excellent way to introduce people to your product or service. You can provide free demonstrations at malls, civic group meetings, residential facilities, and almost anywhere else you can think of. If you have a product and provide free samples to get people to try it, that is the same as a demonstration. Sometimes, a free demonstration is the best and most effective way to get new customers.

DIRECT MAIL

The premise of direct mail is to make an offer to someone through the mail so that they will purchase what you are selling. The mail pieces are sometimes elaborate and sometimes very inexpensive. There have been some very successful direct mail campaigns that just used a letter from the marketer to the buyer. Whatever type of direct mail program you plan to use, make certain it contains these basic components.

The most important part is the letter, then a brochure or catalog. You must then make the proper offer in your letter, meaning that you must entice the buyer to purchase. The best way to do this and improve your success ratio is to have a proper list, which you can purchase from a list broker.

Some other suggestions include hand-writing the envelope instead of mailing labels, sending the material first class with many smaller-valued stamps on the envelope, and creating some sort of involvement with the piece. This can be a scratch-off card, a tear-off coupon, or simply filling out a survey or calling a telephone number for a prize. You can also use a handwritten lift letter, which is a smaller piece of paper with a note that tells the buyer why they should buy, especially if they do not intend to make a purchase. Quite often, lift letters help close the sale.

DIRECT RESPONSE ADVERTISEMENTS

This basic form of direct marketing requires customers to fill out a coupon or card and mail it in or call a special telephone number to order something, receive information, or win a prize. Some even require the purchaser to visit a location or facility. You, as the marketer, are causing the purchaser to make a direct response to your advertising.

Just remember to code each direct response ad with a name or a number so you can track its effectiveness. You do not want to keep spending money on direct response ads that do not make sales for you.

DIRECTORIES

Directories are a good way to list your business and your name for people to see. Directories can be national or local, part of a civic organization or professional group, and they can be used to market your business or services. When people see your name listed over and over again in a directory, it creates a feeling of security on their part because you are perceived as credible. Choose your directories carefully, as not all of them are for everyone.

DISPLAYS

Displays are used a great deal in stores by suppliers to promote their merchandise. They are also used by manufacturers and vendors at trade shows. Displays attract attention to a product and get people to buy that product. Some displays are very elaborate and some are very simple. You must decide on the type of display you want to use and then make it work for you.

Displays can be simple signs, table tops, bulletin boards, and free standing, as you see at major trade shows. The display should be eye catching and informative. Use a display to enhance a sales presentation.

DOOR HANGERS

You know what these are. They are the plastic bags or hooked pieces that people place on your front door knob. While you may not like a door hanger on your front door when you come home, you must admit they attract your attention. They are also fairly inexpensive, as they usually include a flyer that makes a special offer from one or a number of businesses.

You can set up your own door hanger program and have others pay to participate. Just figure out your costs, get other businesses to sign up, and use those monies to pay the people who distribute the door hangers. You may want to use high school students as your representatives.

EXPANDED BUSINESS HOURS

Many companies never work beyond the traditional 8-5. You should make your business convenient and accessible to customers. Quite often, people will do business with someone just because they are open earlier or later.

FAIRS

Fairs come in all types and sizes. There are state, regional and local fairs. There are business fairs and expositions. There are also community display fairs. Your investment is one of time, a display, booth costs, and printed material to give out. You may also want to provide free samples or demonstrations. Your activities at fairs are similar to your work at a trade show.

FLYERS

Flyers are probably the least expensive way to inform the public about your business. Flyers can be used to announce special sales, special events, new products, discounts, to provide coupons, or just to create a visible presence for you in the community. You can use photos or graphics in the flyers to make them more appealing and to get your message across more effectively.

GIFT CERTIFICATES

Gift certificates are often used to attract new customers and to get current customers to purchase more. Print these up and make them available all year long, as well as around the holidays. You can leave the amount off the certificate and just write it in. If you have a big gift certificate program, print the certificates with different amounts. Then, you just have to fill in the person's name.

GIVE AWAYS

Giving something away, such as a sample product or an initial consultation, is an excellent way to attract business. Once someone has tried your product or service, then it is up to you to get and keep them as a customer. Most people are glad to try something for free, but they are reluctant to pay for something new and untried. Consider giving it away to get more back later.

GRAND OPENING

This is very effective if you are a new business. Wait about two to three months after you have opened, work all the bugs out, and then plan your grand opening. Make it interesting, festive, and fun. Invite current and prospective customers. Inform the media about your event to get additional publicity. Give away products, prizes, coupons, gift certificates, and anything else you can think of to get people to try your product or service.

Turn the grand opening into an annual event by making it an open house. Do everything the same way. The goal is to attract new business while keeping your current customers loyal.

GUARANTEES

Guarantees are a great way to differentiate your business from its competitors. Whatever type of guarantee you offer, be it lifetime, money back, or exchange during a certain time period, just make certain that you honor that guarantee. While guarantees can be very attractive to customers, they can also turn customers away if the promise isn't kept.

Your type and length of guarantee tells customers the confidence you have in your business. There will be times when you have to honor many guarantees simultaneously, but the goodwill this generates will be more than worth the investment.

HELP LINES

Many businesses have instituted 800 telephone help lines for their customers. This is very effective and not that expensive, especially if you work on a regional or national basis. You can even establish a local help line.

Train your personnel to answer the questions that customers may have about your business in a courteous and friendly manner. Teach your customers that they can call the help line any time for assistance. It is even better to offer this assistance for free. You will have more people using the line, but they will also start to refer more people to your business because of this service. In this way, the cost of the help line more than pays for itself.

HOST OR HOSTESS

Having a host or hostess depends upon your type of business. This is not a receptionist, but someone who meets and greets people as they enter your business. This person's role is to make the people who do business with you feel at home.

IMAGE

Many companies decide to embark on an image building advertising campaign, only to abandon it because of its cost. Image advertising can be very expensive. Although every business needs a public image, smart companies build their images through the creation of marketing awareness, recognition, credibility, reliability, longevity, and satisfied customers. These companies do not rely heavily on image advertising. They tend to use more public relations, networking, and community visibility than anything else.

INCENTIVES

Incentives have proven very successful in motivating salespeople to achieve greater sales volumes. Incentives can also motivate your staff to perform better, increase productivity, and turn your staff into your best marketing representatives.

Incentives need not always be monetary, but using money rewards in the program helps. Incentives can be gifts, trips, dinners, or anything that is out of the ordinary reward structure for your business. Just develop a program that ties the incentives to performance and reward accordingly.

INSERTS

Inserts, and free-standing inserts, are often used to attract attention to a special offer. They are either attached to some other advertising piece or they are unattached within another piece. Businesses use inserts because they are usually less expensive than traditional advertising. Inserts are often similar to flyers and can also be used as coupon offers.

Inserts are most often used with the print media, including newspapers, magazines, catalogs, newsletters, and almost anything else that is for a customer's use. This form of marketing either can be very effective if it works, or it can be very costly if it does not generate the business.

IN-SERVICE TRAINING

Employee training is one of the most overlooked and underutilized marketing techniques. The training programs are relatively inexpensive when compared to the returns. Training employees to do their jobs better, or cross training them to help out in other areas, makes employees feel that they are more valuable to the company. They will probably produce more and market your company to more customers. Remember that your two best sales staffs include satisfied customers and happy employees.

INTERNS

Interns are a reliable source of quality employees. College students in almost every discipline must complete an internship to graduate. Contact your local college and work with them to develop an internship program through your business.

LEAD BOXES

Everywhere you go, you see lead boxes that invite you to register to win something free. Travel agencies, health clubs and clothing stores work with lead boxes, whose purpose is to generate a mailing list of interested prospects. The most important thing about a lead box program is the follow-up. Make sure that when you collect these lead boxes full of names and telephone numbers, you call these people and try to get them to come into your business. If you do not follow up, you have wasted your time with this type of program.

LEADS CLUBS

Some entrepreneurs have established leads clubs, where noncompeting business owners and salespeople meet on a regular basis to exchange leads with each other. This provides you with a rich source of prospects whom you would otherwise never have known about. Again, the important thing is to follow up on these leads.

LETTERS TO THE EDITOR

Have you ever considered the publicity value of writing a letter to the editor? You can sign it with your name and your company name. Don't make the letter seem like a blatant advertisement for your business. Follow up on a social issue or something the newspaper reported on earlier. Give your opinion or state the position your company has on the issue. Write enough of these and it looks like you have your own column. The result will be increased credibility and visibility.

LEVERAGING

This is a simple marketing tool whereby you ask your customers and suppliers to introduce you to new business. Leveraging works especially well with suppliers, since they do not want to lose your business. You may not realize it, but you leverage yourself every time you ask someone if they know of a possible customer who can benefit from what you offer. Since you do it to friends, family and customers, why not ask your suppliers for the same type of information? You might be surprised at how many of them are willing to help you.

LOGO

Every business should have a logo that identifies you to the public and provides a direct or perceptual message about your business. Make sure it says what you want it to say. If you want your logo to make an impression so people will remember your company name, then create one that will achieve that goal for you.

MAILING LISTS

Mailing lists are an effective direct marketing tool and they are easy and inexpensive to obtain. Many list houses will produce a mailing list for you according to your specifications which lets you target your marketing efforts in a very precise manner.

You can also develop your own in-house mailing list from your customers and shoppers. Then, you can send them periodic information on your business, such as when sales will occur or new items come in. In-house mailing lists are less expensive than purchased lists, but you must be able to keep your in-house list accurate and up-to-date.

MARKET RESEARCH (See Chapter 2)

NAME

If you have nothing else to work with when marketing your business, make certain your name conveys the proper message. Customers should know who you are and what you do simply by seeing your name.

Many business owners like to have their own name, as the company name, in whole or in part. This is very true with professional service providers. You must then consider a longer company name to convey the message, or you can use a subtitle, as we do: Gerson Goodson, Inc.: Marketing and Management Services. Now, everyone we meet knows who we are and what we do.

NEW BUSINESS REQUESTS

Many companies do not grow or do not succeed simply because the owners never asked for new business. Ask your customers to recommend someone they know who can benefit from your product or services.

The way to make this more effective is to describe a potential customer or an ideal customer to your referral source. Sometimes, people who are asked to refer someone can't think of anyone off the top of their head. However, if you describe the characteristics of your desired customer, they will be reminded of someone. All you have to do is ask.

NEWSLETTER

Newsletters are an excellent way to keep in touch with your clients and prospects. Because they are short, newsletters help readers acquire knowledge that they probably otherwise would never receive because they do not have time to read the original sources. Businesses that write newsletters do this to keep in touch with their clients, maintain visibility, and provide a value-added service.

Newsletters can be very elaborate or very simple. If you are just starting a company newsletter, keep it simple. Both sides of an 8.5″ × 11″ page are sufficient to begin with. Lay out your information so it is easy to read and follow. Use a big headline followed by two or three columns. Use only two or three print sizes in the body of the newsletter. All your copy should be one print size and the section headings and subheadings should be another.

Newsletters are a great way to stay in touch and remind clients who you are. The expense of producing a newsletter, especially if you provide it for free, is just a cost of doing business; the return on this investment can be significant.

If you plan to start a newsletter but do not know how, seek help from a professional. Check with a graphic artist, printer, communications specialist, and a public relations or marketing consultant.

NOVELTY ITEMS

These are used to enhance the product or service you are offering. Novelty items are unique toys that people would never buy for themselves but that they would like to have. You provide these novelty items to them as an adjunct to your product or service. The item is basically a memory reinforcer so that customers will remember you when it comes time to purchase again.

OFF PRICING

This marketing technique is used most often when business is slow. Companies tend to advertise an off-price sale to try to move stagnant inventory or to generate revenues. A more effective and less expensive off-price approach would be to send a letter to your current and former customers informing them of a special sale just for them. All products (services) will be reduced in price for a short time as a way of thanking them for their business. You can say that this off-price sale will not be advertised to the public. You will not only generate sales, but you will also generate a great deal of good will and loyalty from your customers.

ONE-MINUTE MESSAGES

This works very well with professional service providers such as physicians, attorneys, and accountants, but it can also be used in retail businesses. The premise is to spend an extra minute with each customer telling them about something that is of interest. It can be a message on health, an upcoming sale, or a new product that will be coming out. The point is to invest one extra minute to market yourself and your business.

PACKAGING

Whether you run a retail business, sell a product, or provide a service, your packaging can make or break you. Not every product can be seen in its box, so the packaging is essential to conveying the message of what is in the box. The packaging has to be inviting and informative enough to get the shopper to buy.

Goods and products can be packaged in a tangible box or in some other format. Services can only be packaged by the image you present. Remember that as you call on your next prospect or client. You are both the packaging and the service rolled into one. Package yourself and your employees well, and you should see an increase in sales.

PER INQUIRY OR PER ORDER ADVERTISING

Many companies simply cannot afford the high costs of advertising. Per inquiry or per order advertising is a method that reduces these costs. You simply work with the advertising medium or supplier and provide them with a specific amount of money or a percentage based on each inquiry or order that you get to your ads. You are essentially paying them from money you may be earning with an inquiry and from money you are definitely earning with an order.

Advertisers may be reluctant not to get their money up front. However, if you convince them that more money could be made with one of these approaches, you may be able to advertise in places and ways you could never have afforded otherwise. Everyone involved in these types of marketing techniques must be able to "see the future," because that is where the payoff is.

PHONE HOLD MESSAGES

Many businesses have to place their customers on hold on the telephone. These businesses also tend to play radio music during that time. What happens if the radio is playing an ad for your competitor? Then, you are paying for your customer or prospect to listen to your competitor's ads.

Phone hold messages play your advertising and marketing messages to customers while they wait on hold. They hear only about your business and nothing else. There are companies that just set up phone hold message systems, or you can call your local telephone company. If you don't take advantage of phone hold messages, don't play anything at all.

PIGGYBACKING

Piggybacking gets you involved with an already successful event or promotion. Many businesses use piggybacking when they work with a charity that has an annual fundraiser. The cost is usually minimal, the visibility is high, and the credibility is instant.

You would usually want to piggyback with a noncompeting business, but sometimes it is beneficial to work with your competitors on a program. Take a look around your community and see if there are any events, programs, or promotions that you can become part of. Even though you will be doing the piggybacking, you still must contribute your time, effort, and some money to the success of the program.

POSITIONING

This is not so much a marketing implementation technique as it is part of the marketing plan and the foundation for all your implementation techniques. Positioning is the place you hold in the minds of your customers compared to your competitors. Are you the market leader or a follower? Do you offer quality service or poor service? Are yours the highest prices or the lowest, or in the middle? Keep in mind that positioning your business properly and then targeting your efforts to support that position will ensure your success.

PREMIUMS

Premiums come in many shapes, sizes, and forms. They are inexpensive, perceived-value add-ons to a regular purchase or they are free gifts to clients, prospects, or employees. Premiums connote extra value, and they are provided as an incentive to continue to do business with a company. In fact, premiums are quite often referred to as premium incentives.

PRESS (MEDIA) KIT

This is essential for any business to have. It does not have to be very expensive, but it must be professional looking.

Your press kit contains information about your company, its key employees, the products or services it offers, and other information that is pertinent or interesting to the media, such as reprints of articles you have written or that have been written about you. The press kit can also contain testimonial letters from satisfied customers and a picture of the person, product, or service you are trying to promote.

The press kit is used whenever you need to send out more information than is covered in a press release or when the media requests more information from you. It is an extension of your corporate image. That is why you must make certain the kit looks very professional. If you cannot develop one yourself, seek the assistance of a marketing or public relations professional.

PRESS RELEASE TOP 10 TOPICS

Here is a list of the top 10 topics that interest editors when you send a press release. Adapt this list or add topics as you get to know your media contacts personally and find out exactly what interests them.

1. Tie-ins with the news of the day.
2. Staging an event.
3. Providing the community with useful information.
4. Forming a committee to solve a problem.
5. Giving away an award or scholarship.
6. Making a prediction about something.
7. Celebrating an opening or an anniversary.
8. Doing something incredible or very special.
9. Giving away food.
10. Any type of success story, especially overcoming hardship.

PRICE COMPETITIVELY

The goal of competitive pricing is not to be the low-cost leader, but to provide perceived value at a competitive price. Quite often, a business selects a price for their product or service without considering the marketplace or its market value. These businesses are usually the first to go out of business.

You must price your products or services to be competitive and to provide a value to the customers. You should then give added service at no charge. Your customers will perceive you as not only a good value, but also as someone they want to do business with.

Sometimes, you just have to be competitively priced and make up the difference in volume. If you are the only business in the marketplace, then you could probably charge reasonably high prices and the customers will pay it. Once other businesses join you, you must become competitive.

PUBLIC SERVICE ANNOUNCEMENTS (PSA'S)

Every radio and television station provides the community with public service announcements. These are free announcements on the air informing the public of a service you are providing. You may be offering to do some community service or charity work, or you may be giving away products or food. Informing the media of these free events and efforts on your part will lead to public service announcements. The resulting visibility and credibility only serve to enhance your business. Use PSA's as wisely and judiciously as you use your press releases.

QUALITY

People are looking for value for their money, and they measure value in the quality of their purchase. You must promise quality, deliver quality, and then deliver more of it. That is the only way to compete on the quality dimension.

RADIO PROGRAMS

Check out your local morning talk show stations. They are often willing to sell time slots to you to air your own radio show. The cost is usually reasonable, and the returns can be extraordinary. Being host of your own radio show gives you instant credibility and the ability to reach a large, highly targeted audience. To make this work, you have to know when and how to promote your own business during the show.

REBATES/REFUNDS

The one thing people love next to getting something for nothing is getting money back. Just look at how many people shop with coupons and send in for rebate offers. If you use a rebate/refund program, make certain you have a way to collect the customer's name, address, and telephone number for your mailing list. Make sure that everyone on your staff is aware of the program, how it works, and what to expect when a rebate or refund is requested. Your staff must also have the authority to make exceptions on the spot without having to get other approvals. This can occur if the redemption date has expired or the rebate program has changed for whatever reason.

RECALL/REACTIVATION PROGRAMS

These are usually mail or telephone programs that try to get former customers back to do more business with you. A recall or reactivation program has to show concern for the customer. The program cannot be a blatant request or demand that they come back to do business with you. Think about what would attract you to a business you used to work with, and then communicate that friendly message to your former customers.

REFERRALS

Every business needs them, but not enough businesses ask for them. Referrals are the heart of every successful business. In fact, many businesses in all fields work strictly on a referral basis.

The first way to build a referral business is to establish a referral network. These are people who will refer to you, and you get them to do that by asking. Describe the potential customer to your referral source. You can't get the business if you do not ask for the business.

Another way to increase referrals is to establish a tiered referral reward system. This rewards current customers as they continue to refer new customers to the business. The more customers referred, the greater the reward. The tiered referral reward system acts as an incentive to continue to do business with you as well as to refer new customers.

REPRINTS

Duplicate any articles that you publish, that are written about you, or that mention your company or your name. Reproduce any ads or advertorials you may use. Send these to prospective and current customers to give them an idea of your business. You can also place these in your media kit.

If you can afford to, take the originals to a printer and have them reproduced professionally. They will look better than photocopies. If the publication sells reprints, take theirs because they all will look like originals.

SALES LETTERS

Sales letters are personalized letters to customers and prospects announcing a sale on your products and services or the introduction of a new product or service. They often contain a discount or value coupon as a call to action for the customer to come in and buy now.

SAMPLING

Sampling is giving away items, tastes, or tries of your product or service. Sampling is often used when a company wants to introduce a new product or service or lure customers from a competitor. People are very willing to take a free sample of something, and if your sample interests them enough, they will possibly switch to what you are selling.

SEARCHLIGHT

A giant searchlight is a fabulous attention getter for your business if you remain open at night or you have a grand opening in the evening. The searchlight lights up the sky and draws people to its source, which is your business. The rental cost is minimal and the number of people it attracts is maximal.

SEMINARS, SPEECHES, AND WORKSHOPS

These are all superb ways to become known in the community, to develop credibility as an expert on the subject, and to become respected for your contribution to the community. You can sponsor your own seminar or workshop, but this can be very costly because of the printing and postage costs associated with flyers, brochures, mailing, and advertising.

You can launch your reputation as a speaker by contacting professional, civic, and social organizations and offering to speak to their membership. The more speeches you give, the more people you will meet. This can translate into more customers for your business. You must also decide whether or not to charge for your speeches. If you are just starting out, donate your time so that you will have an opportunity to get on the programs. As people from one group begin to recommend you to other groups, you can consider charging for your presentation.

SERIAL APPOINTMENTS

This works for physicians, accountants, lawyers, tailors, and anyone else who has to meet a customer on several occasions. Scheduling serial appointments at the time of the initial meeting ''commits'' the customer to continuing to do business with you. When you combine this with confirmation calls, cards or letters, or your recall program, you have a very effective marketing and customer service tool to keep clients coming back to you.

SHOP YOUR COMPETITORS

Most businesses are aware of the need to know what their competitors are doing, but few actually shop them. Shopping your competitors involves going to their place of business, perhaps even spending money there, to see how they price their product or service and handle a customer. Collect brochures, advertisements, and other information about the business, and then identify their weaknesses so you can capitalize on them. The more you know about your competition, the more effective you will be in the marketplace.

SIGNAGE

Many businesses fail because nobody knew where they were located or what they offered. If you have an office or store front where you conduct your business, make sure the signage is visible from the street, is on the building, your windows, and anywhere else you are allowed to place a sign. You may even hang a banner across the building or from poles in your parking lot. You must have a sign that can be read from the street and that directs people to your business. Make certain all your signs comply with building and city codes.

SPONSORSHIPS

Sponsor something: a youth sports team, a race, a special community activity, a fundraiser for a charity, or some other type of event. Your sponsorship is acknowledged on all the printed material associated with the event or league, on the uniforms if it is a team sponsorship, and in the group newsletters. You should also inform the press about your sponsorship as a community contribution.

Sponsorships generate marketing and advertising for your business as well as an enormous amount of good will. People will see your name on a continuous basis, leading to increased familiarity, credibility, and security. They will want to do business with you.

STAMPS

A simple rule of thumb is that if you want to get an envelope opened, use more stamps to equal the required amount of postage. The person who receives your letter will become intrigued by the number of stamps and open your letter just to see who it is from. Consider using special stamps, such as commemorative or scenic stamps. These, too, will arouse interest on a business letter and get the envelope opened.

STUFFERS

Make up a flyer promoting something about your business and place it in the bag of every customer who leaves. Give it to shoppers who do not make a purchase. Contact other businesses and offer to cross promote with them. You will stuff their flyers in your customers' bags if they will stuff yours in their customers' purchases.

TAG LINES

Tag lines are an extra sentence or two tagged (added) on to your radio, television, or print advertisement mentioning a special event or sale. The tag lines are not a regular part of the promotion and should only be used to announce something that is different and unique from your regular business activities. Tag lines can also give a special message to customers, such as saying thank you for the business during a specific period of time. The tag line is virtually a free marketing technique because it is added to advertising that is already paid for.

TAKE-ONE DISPLAYS

Take-one displays are flyers or brochures in a display case that says ''Take one.'' The display should attract attention to the flyer or brochure, which then informs customers of a sale or the benefits of doing business with you. Take-one displays work very well in high-traffic areas where people do not have time to stop for very long, as well as at the checkout counter or cash register. They also work well next to impulse items, because customers tend to buy the impulse item and pick up the material from the display at the same time.

TELEMARKETING

It is less expensive to reach a customer by telephone than in person. You can also reach more people in a given time period.

The key to successful telemarketing is a well-prepared telemarketer. This means having a person who knows your product or service, can follow a well-written script and deviate from it when necessary while keeping the conversation natural, and remains courteous to the customer at all times. While some products or services can sell themselves over the telephone, usually it is the skills of the telemarketer that determine the number and dollar amounts of the sales.

TESTIMONIALS

When a customer tells you they are satisfied with the way you conduct your business or with a purchase they made from you, ask them to write it in a letter. Collect these testimonial letters from as many people as possible. Use them as additional sales and marketing tools. Customers and prospects always like to read about what people like themselves think of doing business with you. These testimonial letters, and even short quotes, will add credibility to what you do.

Keep these letters in protective sheets in a three-ring binder. This way, all your customers can read them without destroying the letters. It also looks very professional to have them in a binder.

TRACKING

Always ask customers where they heard about you or who referred them to you. All ads, flyers, and coupons should have a code on them so you can track them. Developing effective tracking techniques lets you determine the cost of your marketing program and your return on investment. It then allows you to evaluate the program and make revisions, if necessary.

TRADE SHOWS

These are an excellent way to get your message in front of hundreds or thousands of people for very little cost. Of course, you must figure in the expense of the booth, travel, room and board, and salaries of the people attending the trade show. However, it is worth it if you want to reach large numbers of people committed to buying what you market.

Make certain your display is professional and eye catching. Have enough sales literature and business cards to give out and enough people in your booth to talk to prospects as they come by. Make sure you follow up every lead from the trade show with a letter, another brochure, and a telephone call. Almost 25% of the leads obtained at trade shows are never followed up. That is too much business to let go to waste.

T-SHIRTS

T-shirts, like baseball caps, are an excellent way to have your message seen by the public. You can sell or give the shirts or caps away. Just make sure they promote your company and the message and image you want to project. T-shirts and caps are often viewed as a specialty advertising item, but they are effective and many businesses neglect to use this message medium.

UNIQUE SALES PROPOSITION (USP)

The USP differentiates your message from your competitors'. Your USP must be made in conjunction with your unique marketing position (UMP), which positions you in the minds of your consumer. The USP and the UMP combined often determine how successful your business will be.

To determine your USP, ask yourself what it is you are really selling, and see if that is what customers are really buying. If there is a match, write it down. If there is a discrepancy, look at your product or service from the customer's viewpoint. Then, write your USP from that perspective.

VALUE-ADDED SERVICE

Providing value-added service means you will give customers more for their money. You may extend a warranty at no extra charge, make a delivery out of a standard delivery area, or go out of your way to give your customers something extra. You are giving added value (and service) to the purchase they make. Value-added service all but guarantees customers will purchase from you again and refer their family and friends to you. It costs you nothing and gains you a great deal.

VENDOR SUPPORT PROGRAMS (See Co-Op Advertising)

These types of programs are often used with special events, such as a grand opening. You contact your vendors or suppliers, inform them of what you are doing, and ask them to make a financial contribution to the event. In return, you will give them media exposure in your service area through the newspaper, radio, and television ads you will create promoting the event.

Vendors are often quite happy to participate in these programs, which are similar to co-op marketing programs. Vendors state every year that millions of dollars in support and co-op programs go unused because nobody asks them for the funds to participate in these programs.

VOLUNTEER

Volunteer for a community service or charity. Become a member of a service organization, sit on committees or boards, help out with events. Work for a charity. Customers view businesses that volunteer people and products or services in a very favorable light. They often choose to do business with companies just because of their civic-mindedness.

VOLUNTEERS

Don't only be a volunteer, use volunteers. Many people, especially retirees, are eager to volunteer to help a business help people. You can use volunteers to act as hosts or hostesses, guides, customer service people, or in any capacity you can think of. Not only does this help your business, it also creates a favorable image to customers and the general public.

WELCOME WAGON

This can be an effective tool if your product or service warrants being promoted to new homeowners or move-ins. The Welcome Wagon is relatively inexpensive, and someone else delivers the message for you. Usually, you have to provide a coupon with a discount offer to the new neighbor.

This approach is worth trying if your offer is intriguing enough. The Welcome Wagon has both success stories and failures, but it can promote you to newcomers for a relatively inexpensive fee. You will have to try it yourself and track it to see if it is effective.

WORD OF MOUTH

When someone refers you to a friend, they have given you instant credibility. The new customer is much more likely to buy from you than if they had to come in to see you on their own. If you satisfy the new customer, that person will also refer others to you. Your entire business can be built on word-of-mouth marketing.

Word-of-mouth marketing can also hurt your business. Think of a business that does not deliver on its promises or does not sell what it advertises: it can take them up to 10 years to recover.

WRITING

Write and publish articles, books, or monographs. If you cannot find someone to publish these for you, publish them yourself. Published work gives you instant credibility as an expert, and everyone likes to do business with an expert.

YELLOW PAGES

The provider of the Yellow Pages will tell you that every business needs to be listed, and a display ad is better than a line ad, and a large ad is better than a small ad, and red is better than black. The only business that these things are better for is the Yellow Pages provider.

If you use the Yellow Pages as a marketing vehicle, consider the neighborhood directories as well as the regional directory. You must also consider the type of ad you will place. Unique listings can be more effective than large or colorful listings. Create your own category; then you will have no competition.

If you can afford it, you may want to consider multiple line listings in several categories. To determine where you should place your listings, ask your customers where they would look for you if they were to use the Yellow Pages. Then place the listings in the most often recommended categories.

Yellow Pages are effective, when used properly. That means having a professional create your ad in concert with your entire marketing campaign. It also means having the ad sell your business or service, not just give your name and telephone number. Yellow Pages can be a big, ineffective investment. Here again, you must track the business it brings in. If you are paying for a large ad and you are not getting at least a 10:1 return on the investment for that ad, perhaps you should reconsider this as a marketing tool.

ONE FINAL WORD TO THE WISE AND SUCCESSFUL

Plan to market your business in the least expensive, most effective manner possible. It is marketing that drives a business, nothing else. Most businesses do not have the budgets of mega-corporations, yet they can be just as effective in their marketing efforts if they use one or several of these implementation techniques.

Be patient with your marketing program. Give it time to work. Evaluate it carefully and honestly and make changes where necessary. Although these techniques are simple and inexpensive, they will work and your business will improve. Try them. You will be pleasantly surprised. Good luck!

A P P E N D I X

Sales &
Marketing Forms

DAILY SALES CALL REPORT

Salesperson: _____   Calls made/completed: _____

Day/Date: _____   Appointments made: _____

Contact	Company	Address	Telephone	Appt.	Callback	Referral	Comments

WEEKLY SALES CALL SUMMARY

Week Ending	Sales Person	Calls Made	Calls Completed	Appt. Made	Sales	Total Revenues	Action/ Comments

MONTHLY PROSPECT LIST

Salesperson: _____   Month/Year: _____

Contact	Company	Address	Telephone	Old/New	Source	Referred By	Comments

MARKETING INFORMATION TRACKING SHEET

Name	Address	City/St.	Zip	Telephone	Hear About?	Action

COMPETITOR INFORMATION SOURCES

I. Information Supplied by the Competitors, knowingly or unknowingly
 A. Speeches
 B. Direct Observation/On-site Visits
 C. Direct Inquiry
 D. Company Publications
 E. Press Releases/News Stories
 F. Current or Former Employees
 G. Financial Reports/Stock Information
 H. Advertisements
 I. Help Wanted Ads
 J. Correspondence

II. Trade Sources
 A. Trade Publications
 B. Professional/Trade Organizations
 C. Trade Shows
 D. Conventions and Meetings

III. Published Sources
 A. Periodicals/Trade Journals
 B. Directories
 C. Bibliographic and General Reference Works
 D. Electronic Data Bases

IV. Other Sources of Information
 A. Suppliers
 B. Customers
 C. Other Competitors
 D. Distributors
 E. Journalists
 F. Specialists: Accountants, Lawyers, Consultants
 G. Unions
 H. Your Employees Their Friends and the Grapevine
 I. Financial and Security Analysts
 J. University Sources

NOTES

NOTES

NOTES

NOTES

NOW AVAILABLE FROM CRISP PUBLICATIONS

Books • Videos • CD Roms • Computer-Based Training Products

Subject Areas Include:

Management

Human Resources

Communication Skills

Personal Development

Marketing/Sales

Organizational Development

Customer Service/Quality

Computer Skills

Small Business and Entrepreneurship

Adult Literacy and Learning

Life Planning and Retirement

CRISP WORLDWIDE DISTRIBUTION

English language books are distributed worldwide. Major international distributors include:

ASIA/PACIFIC

Australia/New Zealand: In Learning, PO Box 1051 Springwood QLD, Brisbane, Australia 4127
Telephone: 7-3841-1061, Facsimile: 7-3841-1580   ATTN: Messrs. Gordon

Singapore: Graham Brash (Pvt) Ltd. 32, Gul Drive, Singapore 2262
Telphone: 65-861-1336, Facsimile: 65-861-4815   ATTN: Mr. Campbell

CANADA

Reid Publishing, Ltd., Box 69559-109 Thomas Street, Oakville, Ontario Canada L6J 7R4.
Telephone: (905) 842-4428, Facsimile: (905) 842-9327   ATTN: Mr. Reid

Trade Book Stores: Raincoast Books, 8680 Cambie Street, Vancouver, British Columbia, Canada V6P 6M9.
Telephone: (604) 323–7100, Facsimile: 604-323-2600   ATTN: Ms. Laidley

EUROPEAN UNION

England: Flex Training, Ltd. 9-15 Hitchin Street, Baldock, Hertfordshire, SG7 6A, England
Telephone: 1-462-896000, Facsimile: 1-462-892417   ATTN: Mr. Willetts

INDIA

Multi-Media HRD, Pvt., Ltd., National House, Tulloch Road, Appolo Bunder, Bombay, India 400-039
Telephone: 91-22-204-2281, Facsimile: 91-22-283-6478   ATTN: Messrs. Aggarwal

MIDDLE EAST

United Arab Emirates: Al-Mutanabbi Bookshop, PO Box 71946, Abu Dhabi
Telephone: 971-2-321-519, Facsimile: 971-2-317-706   ATTN: Mr. Salabbai

SOUTH AMERICA

Mexico: Grupo Editorial Iberoamerica, Serapio Rendon #125, Col. San Rafael, 06470 Mexico, D.F.
Telephone: 525-705-0585, Facsimile: 525-535-2009   ATTN: Señor Grepe

SOUTH AFRICA

Alternative Books, Unit A3 Sanlam Micro Industrial Park, Hammer Avenue STRYDOM Park, Randburg, 2194 South Africa
Telephone: 2711 792 7730, Facsimile: 2711 792 7787   ATTN: Mr. de Haas